BAKE BAKE BAKE
FOR FOR FOR
RITAIN TAIN

D0563996

KE
R FOR FOR
AIN BRITAIN BRITAIN BI

BAKE BAKE BAKE
FOR FOR FOR
RITAIN BRITAIN BRITAIN

KE BAKE BAKE
R FOR FOR
AIN BRITAIN BRITAIN BI

BAKE BAKE BAKE
FOR FOR FOR
RITAIN BRITAIN BRITAIN

BAKE
FOR
BRITAIN

Summersdale Publishers Ltd
46 West Street
Chichester
West Sussex
PO19 1RP
UK

www.summersdale.com

Printed and bound in the Czech Republic

ISBN: 978-1-84953-267-9

Substantial discounts on bulk quantities of Summersdale
books are available to corporations, professional associations
and other organisations. For details telephone Summersdale
Publishers on (+44-1243-771107), fax (+44-1243-786300) or
email (nicky@summersdale.com).

BAKE
FOR
BRITAIN

summersdale

CONTENTS

INTRODUCTION

Even in difficult times, it is simple pleasures that help us make it through. And what better pleasure is there than the art of baking? From King Alfred the Great's famous failure to watch the cakes to the sponge named for Queen Victoria, Britain's great and good have always loved cakes and baking. As George Orwell rightly said of the English, 'life is unliveable to them unless they have tea and puddings.' The British people have been tempted over the years by the cuisines of France, Italy, Asia and beyond, but still the Great British cake stands tall and continues to reign at teatimes throughout our proud realm.

From the humble fairy cake to the decadent chocolate fudge pudding, there is a cake for every type of baker, and every occasion. For your Queen, for your country, for yourself, take up your rolling pins, wooden spoons and whisks, and Bake for Britain!

TIPS FOR SUCCESSFUL BAKING

- Use the best, freshest ingredients you can to ensure top quality results.
- For best results, use full-fat milk and butter.
- To soften butter, leave it covered and out of the fridge for up to 1 hr. Any longer and it can spoil.
- Eggs should be medium-size.
- Chilled eggs separate more easily than ones at room temperature – so separate them first, and then leave to stand for 20–30 mins to come to room temperature.
- Read through the recipe first, making sure you have all the ingredients and equipment you will need, clean and to hand.
- Make sure all mixing bowls, pans, spoons and utensils are thoroughly cleaned, as oils or soap can affect the outcome of a recipe.

- Preheat the oven thoroughly to ensure even cooking.
- Use the correct size of baking tins or dishes and measure all ingredients accurately.
- Once a cake mixture is ready, transfer it to the baking tin or dish and then into the preheated oven immediately. This is especially important if bicarbonate of soda is used in the recipe as it begins to react immediately.
- Avoid opening the oven door during baking, as this can cause cakes to collapse.
- Allow cakes to cool completely before storing them in airtight containers.

APPLE AND BLACKBERRY CRUMBLE

Serves 4

Ingredients

For the filling

- 25g/1oz butter
- 3 cooking apples, peeled, cored, and sliced
- 150g/5oz caster sugar
- 75g/3oz fresh blackberries

For the crumble

- 110g/4oz plain flour
- 50g/2oz butter, diced
- 50g/2oz caster sugar

Preparation method

Preheat the oven to 180C/350F/Gas 4.

Gently heat the butter in a small pan until melted, then add the apple slices and warm through, until they soften. Add the sugar, and stir well.

Once the sugar has melted, add the blackberries and stir, then remove from the heat.

In a large bowl, sift the flour and add the butter and sugar. Use your fingertips to rub together to create a coarse, breadcrumb texture.

Transfer the filling into a 23cm/9in ovenproof dish. Sprinkle the crumble mixture on top of the filling, making sure you leave no gaps around the sides.

Bake for 20 mins, or until golden brown.

APPLE PIE

Serves 6

Ingredients

For the pastry

- 340g/12oz plain flour
- pinch of salt
- 150g/5oz butter
- 1 tbsp caster sugar
- 1 egg, beaten
- 1 tsp of water

For the filling

- 700g/1½lb cooking apples, peeled, cored and sliced
- juice of ½ lemon
- 110g/4oz sultanas
- 75g/3oz brown sugar
- zest of 1 orange, grated

- pinch of ground cinnamon
- pinch of freshly grated nutmeg
- 1 tbsp milk

To serve
- 1 tbsp caster sugar

Preparation method

Preheat the oven to 200C/400F/Gas 6.

In a large bowl, combine the flour, salt and butter, and rub together until it resembles breadcrumbs. Add the sugar, egg, and a splash of water to form a dough.

Knead on a lightly-floured work surface, then roll out gently. Use two-thirds of the pastry to line a 1 litre/35fl oz pie dish.

In a bowl, sprinkle the apples with the lemon juice, then layer the apples, sultanas, sugar, orange zest, cinnamon and nutmeg in the pie dish.

Use the remaining pastry to form the pie lid, brushing the edges with milk and pressing the edges together. Brush the top with milk, then make a slit in the centre of the pie lid to let steam escape.

Bake for 30 mins, or until golden brown, then sprinkle caster sugar on top and serve.

Of all the several kinds
of sumptuous fare,
There's none that can with
Apple-pye compare,
For costly flavour,
or substantial paste,
For outward beauty,
or for inward taste.

Leonard Welsted, from 'Apple-Pye'

I don't think a really good
pie can be made without
a dozen or so children
peeking over your shoulder
as you stoop to look in at it
every little while.

John Gould

APPLE TURNOVER

Serves 4

Ingredients

- 25g/1oz butter
- 50g/2oz brown sugar
- 1 cooking apple, peeled, cored and sliced
- 25g/1oz raisins
- ½ tsp ground cinnamon
- 4 sheets ready-made filo pastry
- 1 egg, beaten

Preparation method

Preheat the oven to 220C/425F/Gas 7. Lightly grease a baking tray.

Gently heat the butter and sugar in a small pan, then add the apple, raisins and cinnamon and stir well. Remove from the heat when the sugar is dissolved and the apples begin to soften.

Lay out each sheet of pastry and cut into four smaller squares. Place them on the baking tray, then spoon some of the apple mixture into the centre of each square. Brush the edges with the beaten egg, fold over one corner to create a triangle and press the sides together firmly to seal.

Brush the tops of the turnovers with beaten egg.

Bake for 10 minutes.

BAKEWELL TART

Serves 8

Ingredients

For the pastry
- 110g/4oz plain flour
- 75g/3oz butter, diced
- 25g/1oz caster sugar
- pinch of salt
- 1 egg yolk
- 1 tbsp cold water

For the filling
- 150g/5oz butter
- 150g/5oz caster sugar
- 3 eggs, beaten
- 1 egg yolk
- zest of 1 lemon
- 150g/5oz ground almonds

- 2 tbsp raspberry jam
- 1 tbsp flaked almonds

Preparation method

In a large bowl, sift the flour and add the butter, sugar and a pinch of salt, and combine. Add the egg yolk and the water and mix well to form a dough.

Gently flatten the dough into a disc shape, cover with cling film and chill in the fridge for 1 hr.

On a lightly-floured work surface, roll out the pastry thin enough to line a 20cm/8in fluted tart tin, then chill in the fridge for 20 mins.

Preheat the oven to 180C/350F/Gas 4.

Line the tin with the pastry, then line the pastry with baking paper, fill with baking beans, and blind bake for 20 mins, or until light brown. Remove from the oven and allow to cool for 5 mins.

In a bowl, beat the butter and sugar until combined, then add the eggs and egg yolk, lemon zest and ground almonds.

Spread jam on the base of the tart, then pour in the filling mix. Use a spatula to smooth the top.

Bake for 35–40 mins, sprinkling the flaked almonds on top halfway through cooking, until golden brown.

If 3.14 equals pi,
then what is cake?

Carolyn Yang

Cooking is like love. It should be entered into with abandon or not at all.

Harriet Van Horne

BANANA BREAD

Serves 12

Ingredients

- 110g/4oz butter
- 225g/8oz caster sugar
- 2 eggs, beaten
- 4 small ripe bananas, mashed
- 90ml/3fl oz milk
- 1 tsp vanilla extract
- 275g/10oz plain flour
- 1 tsp bicarbonate of soda

Preparation method

Preheat the oven to 180C/350F/Gas 4. Grease a 20cm x 12.5cm/8in x 5in loaf tin.

In a large mixing bowl, beat together the butter and sugar until light and fluffy. Add the eggs, bananas, milk and vanilla extract, and stir well. Sift in the flour and bicarbonate of soda and fold until the mixture until combined.

Transfer the mixture to the loaf tin and bake for 55–60 mins, or until golden brown.

BATTENBERG CAKE

Serves 6

Ingredients

- 150g/5oz butter
- 150g/5oz caster sugar
- 3 eggs, beaten
- 1 vanilla pod, seeds scraped out
- 30ml/1fl oz milk
- 150g/5oz self-raising flour
- 1 tsp pink food colouring
- 75g/3oz apricot jam
- 200g/7oz ready-rolled marzipan

Preparation method

Preheat the oven to 200C/400F/Gas 6. Grease a 15cm/6in square cake tin.

In a large bowl, beat the butter, sugar, eggs, vanilla seeds and milk together. Gradually sift in the flour and continue to beat until smooth.

Divide the mixture equally between two bowls, and add the food colouring to one bowl of mixture, stirring well.

Fold a square of aluminium foil so that it creates a division lengthways down the middle of the cake tin, and covers the bottom. Transfer the plain cake mixture to one side of the tin and the pink cake mixture to the other.

Bake for 30 mins. Place on a wire rack and allow to cool.

Cut both cakes in half lengthways. Take one yellow piece of cake and spread one side with jam, then place one pink piece next to it and press them together. Spread a layer of jam on top of the two pieces of cake, then place the two remaining pieces of cake on top, pink on yellow and yellow on pink. Spread jam all over the top and sides of the cake.

Cut the marzipan so that it's slightly longer than the cake, then wrap it round the cake, pressing gently so that it sticks to the jam. Turn the cake upside down and use a little jam to seal the edges together. Place seal-side down on a serving plate, and chill in the fridge for 30 mins to set.

BRANDY SNAPS

Makes 12

Ingredients

- 110g/4oz butter
- 110g/4oz caster sugar
- 4 tbsp golden syrup
- juice of ½ a lemon
- 110g/4oz plain flour
- 1 tsp ground ginger

Preparation method

Preheat the oven to 180C/350F/Gas 4. Use baking paper to line a large baking tray.

Gently heat the butter, sugar and syrup in a small pan until melted.

Remove from the heat and add the lemon juice. Sift in the flour and ginger. Stir well, and allow to cool.

Use a tablespoon to drop the mixture onto the baking tray, spaced well apart from each other (about 10cm/4in).

Bake for 5–7 mins.

Working as quickly as possible, take each brandy snap, one at a time, and wrap it gently around the handle of the wooden spoon to form the coil shape.

Slide the brandy snap off the handle as soon as it hardens and leave to set.

BREAD AND BUTTER PUDDING

Serves 4

Ingredients

- 25g/1oz butter
- 8 slices of bread
- 50g/2oz sultanas
- 2 tsp ground cinnamon
- 2 eggs
- 25g/1oz caster sugar
- 350ml/12fl oz milk
- 60ml/2fl oz double cream
- 1 tbsp demerera sugar
- 1 tsp freshly grated nutmeg

Preparation method

Grease a 1 litre/35fl oz ovenproof dish.

Spread butter on each slice of bread, cut off the crusts, and cut into triangles.

Place a layer of the bread in the dish, topped with a layer of sultanas and a sprinkling of cinnamon. Repeat this layering process until you have used up all the bread.

In a bowl, crack the eggs and add the caster sugar, then whisk until combined.

Gently warm the milk over a low heat, and pour into the bowl. Add the cream, and stir well to form a custard. Strain if necessary.

Transfer the custard onto the bread pudding, and top with the demerera sugar and the nutmeg. Leave to stand for 30 mins.

Preheat the oven to 180C/350F/Gas 4.

Place the dish in a roasting pan and fill half way up with boiling water. Bake for 35 mins, or until golden brown.

Take away that pudding –
it has no theme.

Winston Churchill

Never spare the Parson's
wine, nor Baker's Pudding.

Benjamin Franklin

BREAD PUDDING

Serves 8

Ingredients

- 500g/1lb 2oz bread
- 500g/1lb 2oz mixed dried fruit
- 75g/3oz mixed peel
- 2 tbsp mixed spice
- 600ml/20fl oz milk
- 2 eggs, beaten
- 150g/5oz muscovado sugar
- zest of 1 lemon
- 110g/4oz butter
- 2 tbsp demerara sugar

Preparation method

In a large mixing bowl, tear the bread into small pieces and add the fruit, mixed peel, mixed spice and milk. Stir well to break up the bread.

Add the beaten eggs, muscovado sugar and lemon zest, and stir. Leave to soak for 15 mins.

Preheat the oven to 180C/350F/Gas 4. Grease a 20cm/8in square cake tin and line with baking paper.

Melt the butter over a low heat, then add to the mixture. Stir well, then transfer to the cake tin. Sprinkle demerara sugar over the top.

Bake for 1½ hrs, or until golden brown. Turn out of the tin and remove the baking paper, then serve.

BUTTERFLY CAKES

Makes 10

Ingredients

For the buns

- 110g/4oz caster sugar
- 110g/4oz butter
- 2 eggs
- 110g/4oz self-raising flour
- ½ tsp baking powder
- 1 tbsp milk

For the jam and buttercream filling

- 50g/2oz butter
- 75g/3oz icing sugar
- 2 tbsp strawberry jam

Preparation method

Preheat the oven to 190C/375F/Gas 5. Line a 10-hole fairy cake tin with paper cases.

In a large bowl, beat together the sugar, butter and eggs until combined. Fold in the flour, add the baking powder and milk, and stir until smooth.

Half-fill each case with the mixture, and bake for 15–20 mins.

Place on a wire rack and allow to cool completely.

For the buttercream, beat together the butter and icing sugar until smooth, leaving some icing sugar aside for dusting.

Using a sharp knife, cut a disc from the top of each cake, and cut each disc in half. Spread jam on top of each cake, then a spoonful of buttercream, and finish by arranging the two halves of leftover cake on the top to resemble butterfly wings. Use the leftover icing sugar to dust the tops.

CARAMEL SLICE

Makes 9

Ingredients

For the shortbread

- 175g/6oz butter
- 75g/3oz caster sugar
- 1 vanilla pod, seeds scraped out
- 225g/8oz plain flour

For the caramel

- 200g/7oz butter
- 400g/14oz condensed milk
- 4 tbsp golden syrup
- 1 tsp sea salt

For the topping

- 340g/12oz milk chocolate

Preparation method

Preheat the oven to 180C/350F/Gas 4. Grease a 20cm/8in square cake tin and line with baking paper.

In a large bowl, use your fingertips to rub together the butter, sugar and vanilla seeds. Sift in the flour and continue rubbing to form a rough dough.

Transfer to the cake tin and press down to compact. Bake for 40 mins, reducing the heat of the oven to 150C/300F/Gas 2 after 10 mins. Allow to cool in the tin.

In a large saucepan, bring the butter, milk, syrup and salt to the boil and simmer for 10 mins. Pour the mixture over the shortbread, then chill in the fridge for 30 mins until hardened.

Gently melt the chocolate in a heatproof bowl over a pan of boiling water. Pour the chocolate over the caramel and chill in the fridge for a further 30 mins, or until set. Cut into squares.

CARROT CAKE

Serves 10–12

Ingredients

For the cake

- 200g/7oz plain flour
- 2 tsp baking powder
- 1 tsp salt
- 1 tsp bicarbonate of soda
- 200g/7oz brown sugar
- 250g/9oz carrots, grated
- 110g/4oz walnuts
- 150ml/5fl oz oil
- 2 eggs, beaten

For the icing

- 110g/4oz butter
- 225g/8oz cream cheese

- 50g/2oz icing sugar
- 1 tsp vanilla extract

To decorate
- 50g/2oz chopped walnuts

Preparation method

Preheat the oven to 160C/320F/Gas 2. Grease a 23cm/9in cake tin.

In a large bowl, sift the flour, baking powder, salt and bicarbonate of soda and stir well. Add the sugar, carrot, walnuts, oil and eggs, and stir until combined.

Transfer to the tin, and bake for 65–70 mins.

Place on a wire rack and allow to cool before removing from the cake tin.

In a small bowl, beat together the butter and cream cheese until light and fluffy. Add the sugar and vanilla extract and stir well.

Spread the icing over the cake using a palette knife, and decorate with the chopped walnuts.

CHELSEA BUNS

Makes 6

Ingredients

For the bread:

- 250g/9oz bread flour
- 2 tsp caster sugar
- 7g/¼oz dried active yeast
- 120ml/4fl oz warm milk
- 25g/1oz butter

For the filling:

- 50g/2oz dark brown sugar
- 50g/2oz butter, diced
- 50g/2oz currants
- 50g/2oz sultanas
- 25g/1oz cut mixed peel

For the glaze:

- 2 tbsp milk

Preparation method

In a large bowl, beat together 75g/3oz of the flour, the sugar, yeast and warm milk until combined. Allow to stand for 30 mins.

In a separate bowl, rub together the butter and remaining flour to resemble breadcrumbs. Transfer to the first mixture, which should now be frothy, and fold together, then knead to form a smooth dough.

Lay a damp tea towel over the bowl and leave to stand for 1 hr.

Knead well. On a lightly-floured work surface, roll out the dough to a 1cm/½in thickness, in a rectangle.

Scatter half of the brown sugar evenly over the dough, then scatter the butter cubes, currants, sultanas and peel over, and top with the remaining sugar. Roll the dough lengthways to form a Swiss roll.

Line a large baking tray with baking paper. Using a sharp knife, cut into six pieces lengthways, and place them, spaced well apart, cut-side down on the tray. Cover again with a damp tea towel and leave to stand for 40 mins.

Meanwhile, preheat the oven to 200C/400F/Gas 6. Brush the buns with a little milk, then bake for 30 mins, or until golden brown.

Nothing seems to please a fly so much as to be taken for a currant, and if it can be baked in a cake and palmed off on the unwary, it dies happy.

Mark Twain

CHERRY AND COCONUT CAKE

Serves 6–8

Ingredients

- 175g/6oz butter
- 175g/6oz sugar
- 3 eggs
- 1 tbsp milk
- 50g/2oz desiccated coconut
- 50g/2oz glacé cherries, chopped
- 110g/4oz self-raising flour

Preparation method

Preheat the oven to 180C/350F/Gas 4. Grease a 20cm x 12.5cm/8in x 5in loaf tin and line with baking paper.

In a large bowl, beat together the butter and sugar, then gradually add the eggs and milk and beat until combined. Stir in the coconut and cherries, leaving some of the cherries aside for decoration, then sift in the flour and fold into the mixture until smooth.

Transfer the mixture to the loaf tin and sprinkle any leftover coconut on top. Bake for 45 mins, adding the leftover cherries as decoration for the last 10 mins.

CHOCOLATE CAKE

Serves 8–10

Ingredients

For the cake

- 150g/5oz butter
- 275g/10oz dark brown sugar
- 3 eggs, beaten
- 225g/8oz plain flour
- 50g/2oz cocoa powder
- 2 tsp baking powder
- ½ tsp bicarbonate of soda
- 225ml/8fl oz milk
- 2 tsp vanilla extract

For the chocolate icing

- 200g/7oz plain chocolate
- 200ml/7fl oz double cream

Preparation method

Preheat the oven to 180C/350F/Gas 4. Grease two 20cm/8in round sandwich tins and line with baking paper.

In a large bowl, beat together the butter and sugar, then gradually add the eggs. Sift in the flour, cocoa powder, baking powder and bicarbonate of soda and and fold to combine. Slowly add the milk and vanilla extract, stirring continuously.

Pour half of the mixture into each tin, and bake for 30 mins. Remove from the oven and allow to cool completely.

Meanwhile, heat the chocolate and cream in a small pan over a low heat until the chocolate is melted, then remove from the heat. Whisk together until smooth and thick. Leave to cool and thicken for 1 hr.

Remove the cakes from their tins. Spread chocolate icing over one cake, then place the other cake on top. Spread the remaining icing over the whole cake with a palette knife.

CHOCOLATE FUDGE PUDDING

Serves 4

Ingredients

For the sponge

- 75g/3oz self-raising flour
- 25g/1oz cocoa powder
- pinch of salt
- 110g/4oz muscovado sugar
- 110g/4oz butter
- 1 tsp vanilla extract
- 2 eggs, beaten
- 2–3 tbsp milk

For the sauce

- 75g/3oz muscovado sugar

- 25g/1oz cocoa powder
- 200ml/7fl oz milk

Preparation method

Preheat the oven to 180C/350F/Gas 4. Grease a 1 litre/35fl oz ovenproof dish.

In a large bowl, sift the flour, and add the cocoa powder and salt.

In a separate bowl, beat the sugar, butter and vanilla extract together until light and fluffy, then gradually add the eggs. Pour this mixture into the first bowl, and fold to combine, adding just enough milk so that the mixture drops easily off the spoon.

For the sauce, mix the sugar and cocoa powder in a small bowl and add the milk, beating until smooth.

Transfer the sponge mixture into the ovenproof dish, then pour the sauce on top.

Bake for 45–60 mins.

CHRISTMAS CAKE

Serves 10–12

Ingredients

- 250g/9oz self-raising flour
- 2 tsp mixed spice
- ½ tsp ground cinnamon
- 1 tsp ground cloves
- 50g/2oz ground almonds
- 340g/12oz each raisins, currants and sultanas
- 50g/2oz mixed peel
- 50g/2oz dried apricots, chopped
- 50g/2oz walnuts, chopped
- 50g/2oz unblanched almonds, chopped
- 250g/9oz butter
- 200g/7oz muscovado sugar
- zest and juice of 1 lemon
- 5 eggs, beaten
- 90ml/3fl oz brandy

Preparation method

Preheat the oven to 150C/300F/Gas 2. Grease a 20cm/8in round cake tin and line with baking paper, then wrap brown paper around the outside of the tin and secure with string.

In a large bowl, sift the flour and add the mixed spice, cinnamon, cloves, almonds, raisins, currants, sultanas, peel, apricots, walnuts and almonds. Stir well.

In a separate bowl, beat the butter and sugar together until light and fluffy, then add the lemon zest and eggs and stir. Add this mixture to the first bowl gradually, adding the lemon juice and brandy and continuing to stir until combined.

Transfer the mixture into the cake tin and bake for 2 hrs. Place a sheet of baking paper over the top and bake for a further 45 mins.

Place on a wire rack and allow to cool completely. If you have prepared the cake several weeks before Christmas you can 'feed' it by creating small holes in the top with a skewer and pouring in 2 tbsps of brandy, or orange juice, every week or two to give it a richer flavour.

CHRISTMAS PUDDING

Serves 6–8

Ingredients

- 340g/12oz sultanas
- 340g/12oz raisins
- 225g/8oz caster sugar
- 225g/8oz suet
- 225g/8oz currants
- 110g/4oz mixed candied peel, chopped
- 110g/4oz plain flour
- 110g/4oz fresh breadcrumbs
- 50g/2oz flaked almonds
- 1 tsp ground cinnamon
- 1 tsp mixed spice
- 1 tsp freshly grated nutmeg

- zest of 1 lemon
- 5 eggs, beaten
- 150ml/5fl oz brandy

Preparation method

Grease two 1 litre/35fl oz pudding basins.

In a large bowl, mix together all the dry ingredients, then add the eggs and the brandy and mix well to combine.

Transfer the mixture into the two basins, and cover each with a circle of baking paper, then with aluminium foil on top of that. Tie with string to secure.

Simmer the basins in a large, covered pan for 5–6 hrs, topping up the water so it stays at a constant level, halfway up the basins, throughout the cooking time.

Allow the puddings to mature for 30 days, storing with fresh baking paper and aluminium foil tied around it and in an airtight container. When ready to eat, steam for a further 2 hrs and serve hot.

Oh, a wonderful pudding!
Bob Cratchit said, and
calmly too, that he regarded
it as the greatest success
achieved by Mrs. Cratchit
since their marriage.

Charles Dickens, *A Christmas Carol*

I feel a recipe is only a
theme, which an intelligent
cook can play each time
with a variation.

Jehane Benoît

COFFEE AND WALNUT CAKE

Serves 10–12

Ingredients

For the cake

- 225g/8oz butter
- 225g/8oz caster sugar
- 4 eggs, beaten
- 60ml/2fl oz strong coffee
- 80g/3oz walnuts
- 225g/8oz self-raising flour

For the buttercream icing

- 150g/5oz butter
- 200g/7oz icing sugar
- 60ml/2fl oz strong coffee

To decorate
- walnut halves

Preparation method

Preheat the oven to 180C/350F/Gas 4. Grease two 20cm/8in cake tins and line with baking paper.

In a large bowl, beat together the butter and sugar, then gradually add the eggs until combined. Add the coffee and walnuts and sift in the flour and fold to combine.

Transfer the mixture into the cake tins and bake for 30 mins.

Place on a wire rack and allow to cool completely.

Meanwhile, in a small bowl, beat together the butter and sugar for the icing, until light and fluffy. Add the coffee and stir well.

Spread the buttercream icing over one cake, then place the other cake on top. Spread the remaining icing on top of the second cake with a palette knife. Decorate with the walnut halves.

CORNFLAKE CAKES

Makes 12–15

Ingredients

- 225g/8oz plain or milk chocolate
- 2 tbsp golden syrup
- 50g/2oz butter
- 75g/3oz cornflakes

Preparation method

Line a 12-hole fairy cake tin with paper cases.

Break the chocolate into small chunks and place in a bowl over a small pan of simmering water. Add the syrup and butter, and stir until smooth.

Remove from the heat and add the cornflakes (or other cereal). Stir well to coat the cereal, then transfer spoonfuls at a time to the paper cases.

Chill in the fridge for 1 hr.

CORNISH FAIRINGS

Makes 18–20

Ingredients

- 225g/8oz plain flour
- ½ tsp salt
- 2 tsp baking powder
- 2 tsp bicarbonate of soda
- 2 tsp ground mixed spice
- 3 tsp ground ginger
- 1 tsp ground cinnamon
- 110g/4oz butter
- 110g/4oz caster sugar
- 4 tbsp golden syrup

Preparation method

Preheat the oven to 200C/400F/Gas 6. Grease a large baking tray and line with baking paper.

In a large bowl, sift the flour and add the salt, baking powder, bicarbonate of soda, mixed spice, ginger and cinnamon. Stir well, then add the butter and sugar and rub together with your fingertips until it resembles breadcrumbs.

Gently heat the syrup in a small pan, then add to the bowl and stir until combined.

Roll the mixture into small balls, and place on the baking tray, spread well apart.

Bake for 10–12 mins.

When I cannot write a poem,
I bake biscuits and feel just
as pleased.

Anne Morrow Lindbergh

Cookies are made of
butter and love.

Norwegian proverb

DUNDEE CAKE

Serves 18–20

Ingredients

For the cake

- 150g/5oz butter
- 150g/5oz caster sugar
- 3 eggs, beaten
- 225g/8oz plain flour
- 1 tsp baking powder
- 175g/6oz currants
- 175g/6oz sultanas
- 50g/2oz glacé cherries, halved
- 2 tbsp ground almonds
- 50g/2oz mixed candied peel, chopped
- zest of 1 orange, grated
- zest of 1 lemon, grated
- 1 tbsp milk

To decorate
- 50g/2oz flaked almonds

Preparation method

Preheat the oven to 170C/330F/Gas 3. Grease a 20cm/8in round cake tin and lightly dust with flour.

In a large bowl, beat together the butter and sugar until light and fluffy, then gradually add the eggs, beating to combine.

Fold in the flour, baking powder, currants, sultanas, cherries, almonds, peel and zests, and mix well. Add a splash of milk if necessary.

Transfer the mixture into the tin. Decorate the top with the flaked almonds. Bake for 75 mins, then place on a wire rack and allow to cool completely before removing from the tin.

ECCLES CAKES

Makes 12

Ingredients

For the filling
- 25g/1oz butter, melted
- 150g/5oz light brown sugar
- 175g/6oz currants
- pinch of ground cinnamon
- pinch of freshly grated nutmeg
- zest of ½ orange

For the cakes
- 300g/11oz ready-rolled puff pastry
- 30ml/1fl oz water
- 30ml/1fl oz milk
- 25g/1oz caster sugar

Preparation method

Preheat the oven to 180C/350F/Gas 4.

In a large bowl, mix the butter, sugar, currants, cinnamon, nutmeg and zest until combined.

On a lightly-floured work surface, gently roll out the pastry to a thickness of about ½cm/¼in, and cut into 13cm/5in rounds.

Place a large spoonful of the mixture into the centre of half of the rounds. Brush water around the edges of the pastry, and place another round on top, pressing down at the edges to seal.

Make a slit in the top of each cake with a sharp knife. Brush the tops with milk and sprinkle the caster sugar on top. Place on a baking tray.

Bake for 10–12 mins, or until golden brown.

EGG CUSTARD TART

Serves 10–12

Ingredients

For the pastry case
- 500g/1lb 2oz shortcrust pastry
- freshly grated nutmeg

For the egg custard
- 4 eggs
- 150g/5oz caster sugar
- 300ml/10fl oz double cream
- 300ml/10fl oz milk
- 1 vanilla pod, seeds scraped out

Preparation method

Preheat the oven to 200C/400F/Gas 6.

On a lightly-floured work surface, roll out the pastry to 1cm/½in thickness. Sprinkle half of the nutmeg over the top, fold the dough in half, then roll out again to the same thickness.

Line a 20cm/8in sandwich tin with the pastry and chill in the fridge for 10 mins.

Line the pastry with baking paper, fill with baking beans, and blind bake for 20 mins. Remove the baking paper and beans and return to the oven for a further 15 mins, or until golden brown.

Reduce the heat of the oven to 150C/300F/Gas 2. Tidy the edges of the pastry using a sharp knife.

In a large bowl, whisk the eggs and sugar together.

Gently heat the cream, milk and vanilla pod and seeds in a small pan until it comes to the boil. Slowly pour the mixture into the bowl, whisking it all together. Once combined, use a sieve to strain off the vanilla seeds, then pour the mixture into the tart, filling to the top.

Sprinkle the remaining nutmeg on top of the tart, and bake for 1 hr, or until light brown on top. Place on a wire rack to cool.

FAIRY CAKES

Makes 24

Ingredients

For the cakes
- 110g/4oz butter
- 110g/4oz caster sugar
- 2 eggs, beaten
- 1 tsp vanilla extract
- 110g/4oz self-raising flour
- 2 tbsp milk

For the icing
- 300g/11oz icing sugar
- 1 tbsp warm water
- 2–3 drops food colouring

Preparation method

Preheat the oven to 180C/350F/Gas 4. Line two 12-hole fairy cake tins with paper cases.

In a large bowl, beat together the butter and sugar until light and fluffy. Gradually add the eggs and vanilla extract, and beat until combined.

Sift in the flour and fold mixture to combine, then stir in the milk.

Half-fill each case with the mixture, and bake for 10 mins, or until golden brown.

Place on a wire rack and allow to cool.

For the icing, pour the icing sugar into a small bowl and gradually add drops of water, stirring until smooth, then add the food colouring. Spoon the icing over the cakes and leave to set.

Where there is cake,
there is hope. And there
is always cake.

Dean Koontz

Cooking is at once child's play and adult joy. And cooking done with care is an act of love.

Craig Claiborne

FLAPJACKS

Makes 12

Ingredients

- 175g/6oz butter
- 175g/6oz golden syrup
- 175g/6oz muscovado sugar
- 340g/12oz porridge oats

Preparation method

Preheat the oven to 150C/300F/Gas 2. Grease a 20cm/8in square baking tin and line with baking paper. Melt the butter in a small pan over a low heat, then gradually add the sugar and syrup and stir until the sugar is dissolved.

Remove from the heat, then add in the porridge oats and mix well.

Transfer the mixture to the baking tin and use a wooden spoon to compact.

Bake for 40 mins and allow to cool before cutting into squares or slices.

FRUIT AND NUT SQUARES

Makes 12

Ingredients

- 450g/1lb cooking apples, peeled, cored and diced
- 5 tbsp apple juice
- 225g/8oz mixed dried fruit
- 110g/4oz mixed chopped nuts
- 75g/3oz porridge oats
- 50g/2oz pumpkin seeds
- 2 tbsp vegetable oil
- 75g/3oz self-raising flour

Preparation method

Preheat the oven to 160C/320F/Gas 2. Grease a 15cm/6in square baking tray.

Gently heat the apples and apple juice in a small pan until softened. Remove from the heat and mash. Transfer to a large bowl.

Add the mixed fruit, nuts, oats, pumpkin seeds and oil, and mix well. Sift in the flour and stir until combined.

Transfer to the baking tray and bake for 40 mins. Cut into squares while still warm.

GINGER CAKE

Serves 6–8

Ingredients

- 250g/9oz self-raising flour
- 2 tsp ground ginger
- ½ tsp ground cinnamon
- 1 tsp bicarbonate of soda
- pinch of salt
- 200g/7oz golden syrup
- 2 tbsp syrup from a jar of stem ginger
- 110g/4oz butter
- 50g/2oz preserved stem ginger, diced
- 2 tbsp sultanas
- 110g/4oz muscovado sugar
- 2 eggs, beaten
- 250ml/9fl oz milk

Preparation method

Preheat the oven to 180C/350F/Gas 4. Grease a 20cm/8in square cake tin and line with baking paper.

In a large bowl, sift the flour and add the ground ginger, cinnamon, bicarbonate of soda and salt.

Gently heat the syrup, ginger syrup and butter in a small pan. Add the stem ginger, sultanas and sugar, and stir over a low heat.

Remove from the heat and pour into the bowl, stirring until smooth. Gradually beat in the eggs and the milk.

Transfer to the cake tin and bake for 40 mins.

GINGERBREAD MEN

Makes 10

Ingredients

- 340g/12oz plain flour
- 1 tsp bicarbonate of soda
- 1 tsp ground cinnamon
- 2 tsp ground ginger
- 110g/4oz butter
- 175g/6oz light brown sugar
- 1 egg
- 4 tbsp golden syrup

Preparation method

Preheat the oven to 180C/350F/Gas 4. Line a baking tray with baking paper.

Sift the flour into a bowl, add the bicarbonate of soda, cinnamon and ginger, and stir.

Beat in the butter and sugar.

In a separate bowl, beat the egg with the golden syrup, then add this to the mixture until it forms a dough.

Knead the dough on a lightly-floured work surface until smooth, then wrap in cling film and chill in the fridge for 20 mins.

Roll out the dough and cut out the gingerbread men with a cutter. Place them on the baking tray, leaving about 2in/5cm between each biscuit.

Bake for 15 mins, or until golden brown.

HOT CROSS BUNS

Makes 12

Ingredients

For the buns

- 450g/1lb plain flour
- 1 tsp salt
- 1 tsp ground cinnamon
- 1 tsp mixed spice
- 50g/2oz butter
- 75g/3oz currants
- 50g/2oz mixed peel, chopped
- 7g sachet or 1½ tsp fast-action dried yeast
- 90ml/3fl oz warm water
- 90ml/3fl oz warm milk
- 1 egg, beaten

For the decoration

- 1 egg, beaten
- 110g/4oz shortcrust pastry
- 2 tbsp orange juice
- 2 tbsp granulated sugar

Preparation method

Line a baking tray with baking paper.

Sift the flour into a bowl, add the salt, cinnamon and mixed spice, and stir.

Beat in the butter, then add the currants, mixed peel and yeast. Make a well in the middle of the mixture and add the water, milk and egg, then fold together to make a dough.

Knead the dough on a lightly-floured work surface until smooth. Grease a large bowl and leave the dough in it to rise, covered with a damp tea towel.

After 1 hr, knead the dough again, then separate into 12 pieces. Shape them into buns and place on the baking tray, evenly spaced. Cover again, and leave for a further 45 mins.

Preheat the oven to 200C/400F/Gas 6.

Use the beaten egg to glaze the buns, then use strips of the pastry to decorate.

Bake for 15 mins, or until golden brown.

Gently heat the orange juice and sugar in a small pan until the sugar dissolves. Remove the buns from the oven, brush with the glaze, and place on a wire rack to cool.

Under certain circumstances there are few hours in life more agreeable than the hour dedicated to the ceremony known as afternoon tea.

Henry James,
The Portrait of a Lady

JAM ROLY POLY

Serves 6

Ingredients

For the sponge
- 3 eggs
- 75g/3oz caster sugar
- 75g/3oz self-raising flour

For the filling
- 75g/3oz raspberry jam
- 120ml/4fl oz whipped double cream

To serve
- icing sugar

Preparation method

Preheat the oven to 200C/400F/Gas 6. Grease a 23cm x 30cm/9in x 12in baking tin and line with baking paper. In a large bowl, whisk the eggs and sugar until pale and fluffy. Gently fold in the flour using a palette knife, then transfer to the tin.

Bake for 7–10 mins, then remove from the oven and turn out the sponge onto another sheet of baking paper. Allow to cool for 10 mins.

Spread the jam evenly over the sponge, and then add an even layer of cream, making sure there is a small gap around the edges. Roll the sponge from the short end like a Swiss roll, to form the roly poly shape, then dust with icing sugar.

JAM TARTS

Makes 12–16

Ingredients

- 150g/5oz plain flour
- pinch of salt
- 75g/3oz butter, diced
- 50g/2oz caster sugar
- 1 egg yolk
- 1 tbsp cold water
- Jam of your choice

Preparation method

Preheat the oven to 190C/375F/Gas 5. Grease a 12–16-hole tart tray.

In a large bowl, sift the flour and add the butter and salt. Rub together using your fingertips until it resembles breadcrumbs.

Add the sugar and egg yolk and stir well. Add water if necessary to form a dough.

Knead the dough gently, then wrap in cling film and chill in the fridge for 15 mins.

On a lightly-floured work surface, roll out the pastry to a ½cm/¼in thickness. Cut into rounds to slightly overfill the holes in the tray, and press one into each hole.

Put spoonfuls of jam into each pastry case, making sure they are not overfilled.

Bake for 15–18 mins, or until golden brown.

By the way, we never
eat anyone's health,
always drink it. Why should
we not stand up now and
then and eat a tart to
somebody's success?

Jerome K. Jerome

The Queen of Hearts, she
made some tarts,
All on a summer day:
The Knave of Hearts, he
stole those tarts,
And took them quite away!

Lewis Carroll,
Alice's Adventures in Wonderland

KENTISH COBNUT CAKE

Serves 10–12

Ingredients

- 225g/8oz self-raising flour
- 1 tsp ground ginger
- 110g/4oz butter
- 110g/4oz brown sugar
- 50g/2oz Kentish cobnuts, roasted and chopped
- 1 egg, beaten

Preparation method

Preheat the oven to 180C/350F/Gas 4. Grease a 23cm x 10cm/9in x 4in loaf tin.

In a large bowl, sift the flour and add the ginger and butter. Rub together using your fingertips until it resembles breadcrumbs.

Add the sugar, nuts and egg and stir well. Transfer to the loaf tin.

Bake 25–30 mins.

LEMON DRIZZLE CAKE

Serves 8–10

Ingredients

- 225g/8oz butter
- 225g/8oz caster sugar
- zest of 2 lemons
- 4 eggs, beaten
- 1 tsp baking powder
- 225g/8oz self-raising flour
- juice of 2 lemons
- 110g/4oz icing sugar

Preparation method

Preheat the oven to 180C/350F/Gas 4. Grease a 20cm/8in round cake tin and line with baking paper.

In a large bowl, beat together the butter and sugar until light and fluffy. Add the lemon zest, eggs and baking powder, stirring well, then sift in the flour and fold until well combined.

Transfer the mixture to the cake tin and bake for 75 mins.

While the cake is cooling in its tin, mix together the lemon juice and icing sugar. Using a skewer or fork, prick the warm cake all over, then pour over the lemon and sugar mix.

Leave the cake in the tin until completely cool before removing from the tin and serving.

LEMON MERINGUE PIE

Serves 6–8

Ingredients

For the pastry

- 225g/8oz plain flour
- pinch of salt
- 110g/4oz butter, diced
- 2 tsp caster sugar
- 1 egg yolk
- 1 tsp water

For the lemon curd

- 110g/4oz caster sugar
- 7 tbsp cornflour
- 60ml/2fl oz water

- zest and juice of 4 lemons
- 6 egg yolks
- 110g/4oz butter, melted

For the meringue
- 6 egg whites
- 300g/11oz caster sugar

Preparation method

In a large bowl, sift the flour and add the salt and butter. Rub together using your fingertips until the mixture resembles breadcrumbs. Add the sugar and egg yolk, and mix, adding a splash of water if necessary, to form a dough.

Wrap the dough in cling film and chill in the fridge for 30 mins.

Preheat the oven to 190C/375F/Gas 5. Grease a 23cm/9in tart tin.

On a lightly-floured work surface, gently roll out the pastry thin enough to line the tin, with excess pastry over the sides.

Line the pastry with baking paper, fill with baking beans, and blind bake for 15 mins. Remove the baking paper and beans and return to the oven for a further 5 mins, or until golden brown.

Reduce the heat of the oven to 150C/300F/Gas 2. Tidy the edges of the pastry using a sharp knife.

In a large bowl, mix the sugar and cornflour with enough water so that it forms a paste.

Gently heat the rest of the water with the lemon zest in a small pan until it comes to the boil, then pour into the bowl and whisk to combine. Beat in the lemon juice, egg yolks, and butter. Pour back into the pan.

Heat gently until the mixture thickens, then pour into the pastry case and leave to stand for 5 mins.

In a large bowl, whisk the egg whites vigorously until they form peaks, then gradually add the sugar, whisking all the time. Transfer the meringue onto the lemon curd, and bake for 40 mins.

'Tis an ill cook that cannot
lick his own fingers.

William Shakespeare,
Romeo and Juliet

MADEIRA CAKE

Serves 10–12

Ingredients

- 175g/6oz butter
- 175g/6oz caster sugar
- 3 eggs, beaten
- 1 tbsp milk
- 250g/9oz self-raising flour
- zest and juice of 1 lemon

Preparation method

Preheat the oven to 180C/350F/Gas 4. Grease an 18cm/7in round cake tin and line with baking paper.

In a large bowl, beat together the butter and sugar until pale and fluffy. Gradually add the eggs and milk and continue to stir.

Sift in the flour and fold in the lemon zest and juice, folding until combined.

Transfer to the cake tin and bake for 35–40 mins, or until golden brown.

MALT LOAF

Serves 24

Ingredients

- 150ml/5fl oz hot black tea
- 175g/6oz malt extract
- 75g/3oz muscovado sugar
- 300g/11oz mixed dried fruits
- 2 eggs, beaten
- 250g/9oz plain flour
- 1 tsp baking powder
- ½ tsp bicarbonate of soda

Preparation method

Preheat the oven to 150C/300F/Gas 2. Grease a 900g/2lb loaf tin and line with baking paper.

In a large bowl, combine the hot tea with the malt extract, sugar and dried fruit. Gradually add the eggs and sift in the flour, stirring well. Add the baking powder and bicarbonate of soda, stir vigorously, then spoon the mixture into the tin.

Bake for 75–90 mins. Pierce with a skewer to test; when the skewer comes out clean, the cake is ready.

MARBLE CAKE

Serves 6–8

Ingredients

- 225g/8oz butter
- 225g/8oz caster sugar
- 4 eggs, beaten
- 225g/8oz self-raising flour
- 3 tbsp milk
- 1 tsp vanilla extract
- 2 tbsp cocoa powder

Preparation method

Preheat the oven to 180C/350F/Gas 4. Grease a 20cm/8in cake tin and line with baking paper.

In a large bowl, beat together the butter and sugar, then gradually add the eggs, stirring continuously. Sift in the flour and fold into the mixture, then stir in the milk.

Pour half of the mixture into a separate bowl, and add the cocoa powder to one half, stirring well.

Alternate spoonfuls of each mixture into the cake tin, then use a skewer to swirl the mixture around within the tin to marble.

Bake for 50 mins.

MINCE PIES

Makes 12–16

Ingredients

- 225g/8oz plain flour
- 150g/5oz butter, diced
- 50g/2oz caster sugar
- zest of 1 orange
- pinch of salt
- 1 egg yolk
- 2 tsp water
- 275g/10oz mincemeat
- 1 egg, beaten
- 2 tbsp icing sugar

Preparation method

Preheat the oven to 200C/400F/Gas 6. Grease a 12–16-hole tart tray.

In a large bowl, using your fingertips, rub together the flour, butter and sugar. Add the orange zest and salt and stir well.

Add the egg yolk and water and stir until combined. Wrap in cling film and chill in the fridge for 30 mins.

On a lightly-floured work surface, gently roll the pastry out to 2mm/⅒in thick, and cut into rounds to slightly overfill the holes in the tray, and press one into each hole.

Place a few spoonfuls of mincemeat into the centre of each pie, and form lids from the leftover pastry using shaped pastry cutters. Brush the tops with the beaten egg.

Bake for 12–15 mins. Place on a wire rack and allow to cool, then dust with icing sugar.

Cookery is become an art, a noble science: cooks are gentlemen.

Robert Burton,
The Anatomy of Melancholy

Though we eat little flesh
and drink no wine,
Yet let's be merry;
we'll have tea and toast;
Custards for supper,
and an endless host
Of syllabubs and jellies
and mince-pies...

**Percy Bysshe Shelley,
from 'Letter to Maria Gisborne'**

OXFORD PUDDING

Serves 4

Ingredients

- 300g/11oz ready-made puff pastry
- 10 apricots
- 2 tbsp sugar
- 6 eggs
- 60ml/2fl oz double cream
- 2 egg whites

Preparation method

Preheat the oven to 220C/425F/Gas 7. Grease a 23cm/9in pie dish and line with the pastry.

Steam the apricots until tender, then dice, adding sugar to taste. Leave to cool.

Beat the eggs and double cream until smooth and pour over the cooled apricots. Transfer the mixture to the pie dish.

Bake for 30 mins, turning the oven down to 180C/350F/Gas 4 after 15 mins.

Beat the two egg whites, combining with the leftover sugar. Pour this topping over the baked pie and cook for a further 10 mins.

PLUM AND PEAR COBBLER

Serves 4–6

Ingredients

For the filling

- 450g/1lb plums, stoned and quartered
- 450g/1lb pears, peeled, cored and sliced
- 75g/3oz muscovado sugar
- ½ tsp freshly grated nutmeg
- ½ tsp ground cinnamon

For the topping

- 50g/2oz butter
- 225g/8oz self-raising flour
- 25g/1oz caster sugar
- 90ml/3fl oz milk

Preparation method

Preheat the oven to 200C/400F/Gas 6.

Gently simmer the plums, pears, sugar, nutmeg and cinnamon in a small pan over a low heat until the pears soften. Transfer to an ovenproof dish.

In a large bowl, beat together the butter and flour. Gradually add the sugar and milk, stirring well to form a dough.

On a lightly-floured work surface, roll out the dough to a 1cm/½in thickness, and cut into rounds.

Place the rounds on top of the pear and plum filling and brush with milk.

Bake for 20 mins, or until golden brown.

RICE PUDDING

Serves 4

Ingredients

- 50g/2oz butter
- 110g/4oz pudding rice
- 75g/3oz caster sugar
- 1 litre/35fl oz milk
- 150ml/5fl oz double cream
- 1 tsp vanilla extract
- freshly grated nutmeg

Preparation method

Preheat the oven to 140C/275F/Gas 1.

Gently heat the butter in a large casserole dish over a medium heat until melted, then stir in the rice and sugar.

Once the sugar has dissolved and the rice has swollen, add the milk, cream and vanilla extract and stir until smooth. Bring to the boil, then add the nutmeg and stir again.

Bake for 60–75 mins, covering with a lid for the last 15 mins.

ROCK CAKES

Makes 8

Ingredients

- 225g/8oz self-raising flour
- ½ tsp ground mixed spice
- ½ tsp ground cinnamon
- 110g/4oz butter
- 110g/4oz demerara sugar
- 50g/2oz sultanas
- 50g/2oz currants
- 1 egg, beaten
- 1 tbsp milk

Preparation method

Preheat the oven to 180C/350F/Gas 4. Line a baking tray with baking paper.

In a large bowl, sift the flour and add the mixed spice and cinnamon. Rub in the butter using your fingertips, then add the sugar, currants and sultanas and mix well. Add the egg and combine to form a dough. Add a splash of milk if necessary.

Use a wooden spoon to place large dollops of the dough on the baking tray, then sprinkle with sugar.

Bake for 10–12 mins, or until golden brown.

Too many cooks, in baking
rock cakes, get misled by
the word 'rock'.

P. G. Wodehouse

Peter Careful had a cake
Which his kind mamma did bake;
Of butter, eggs, and currants made,
And sent to Peter – carriage paid.

**Elizabeth Turner,
from 'Peter's Cake'**

SCONES

Makes 6

Ingredients

- 225g/8oz self-raising flour
- 1 tsp baking powder
- 2 tbsp caster sugar
- 50g/2oz butter, diced
- 1 egg, beaten
- 90ml/3fl oz milk

To serve
- clotted cream
- strawberry jam

Preparation method

Preheat the oven to 200C/400F/Gas 6. Line a baking tray with baking paper.

In a large bowl, combine the flour, baking powder and sugar. Rub in the butter until the mixture resembles breadcrumbs.

Make a well in the centre and add the egg and milk, leaving a small amount of the milk aside. Stir the mixture together and knead on a lightly-floured work surface until the dough is smooth.

Press out the dough to 2½cm/1in thick, and cut into rounds using a biscuit cutter. Place on the baking tray and brush the tops with the leftover milk to glaze.

Bake for 10–12 mins, or until golden brown. Place on a wire rack to cool. Serve with clotted cream and strawberry jam.

SCOTCH PANCAKES

Serves 2–4

Ingredients

For the pancakes

- 2 tbsp sunflower oil
- 110g/4oz self-raising flour
- 2 eggs
- 90ml/3fl oz milk
- 2 tbsp icing sugar

To serve

- 2 tbsp maple syrup

Preparation method

Preheat a large heavy-bottomed frying pan. Brush with
the sunflower oil.

In a large bowl, sift the flour and gradually add the eggs
and milk, whisking continuously until smooth. Add the
icing sugar, and whisk to combine.

Transfer the mixture to the frying pan, large spoonfuls
at a time. Cook each for 1–2 mins on each side, or until
light golden brown.

Drizzle the maple syrup over the cooked pancakes.

SHOEBURYNESS PUDDING

Serves 4

Ingredients

- 75g/3oz caster sugar
- 2 eggs, separated
- 25g/1oz self-raising flour
- 50g/2oz butter
- 300ml/10fl oz milk
- pinch of salt

Preparation method

Preheat the oven to 180C/350F/Gas 4. Grease a 15cm/6in ovenproof dish.

In a large bowl, beat together the sugar, egg yolks, flour, butter, milk and salt to form a batter.

Whisk the egg whites until they form stiff peaks, then gradually fold into the mixture.

Transfer to the ovenproof dish, place the dish inside a large roasting tray, and fill the tray with boiling water.

Bake for 40 mins, or until light golden brown.

SHORTBREAD

Makes 20

Ingredients

- 110g/4oz butter
- 50g/2oz caster sugar
- 110g/4oz plain flour
- 50g/2oz rice flour

Preparation method

Heat the oven to 190C/375F/Gas 5. Line a baking tray with baking paper.

Beat the butter and the sugar together in a bowl until smooth, then add the plain flour and rice flour, stirring to form a paste.

Place on a lightly-floured work surface and gently roll out the paste to approx. 1cm/½in thick.

Cut into fingers and place on the tray. Sprinkle with icing sugar and chill in the fridge for 20 mins.

Bake in the oven for 15–20 mins, or until light golden brown.

Shortbread has beneficial
effects on the soul.

Lucy Ellmann, *Sweet Desserts*

A compromise is the art of
dividing a cake in such a
way that everyone believes
he has the biggest piece.

Ludwig Erhard

SIMNEL CAKE

Serves 10–12

Ingredients

- 225g/8oz self-raising flour
- 225g/8oz butter
- 225g/8oz muscovado sugar
- 4 eggs, beaten
- 110g/4oz glacé cherries
- 225g/8oz sultanas
- 110g/4oz currants
- 50g/2oz mixed candied peel, chopped
- zest of 2 lemons, grated
- 2 tsp ground mixed spice
- 450g/1lb marzipan
- 1–2 tbsp apricot jam
- 2 tbsp milk

Preparation method

Preheat the oven to 150C/300F/Gas 2. Grease a 20cm/8in cake tin and line with baking paper.

In a large bowl, sift the flour and add the butter, sugar, eggs, cherries, sultanas, currants, peel, zest and mixed spice, beating until combined. Transfer half of the mixture into the cake tin.

Roll out the marzipan and divide into three large balls. Use one ball to form a round, and place on top of the cake mixture in the tin. Pour the rest of the cake mixture on top of the marzipan.

Bake for 2½ hrs, covering with aluminium foil after 1 hr. Place on a wire rack and allow to cool completely. Preheat the grill to high.

Gently heat the apricot jam over a low heat and spread over the top of the cake. Use one marzipan ball to form a round and place on top of the cake, pressing down to seal. Brush the top with milk, then divide the remaining marzipan ball into eleven smaller balls, and arrange around the edge of the cake. Brush these with milk too, then place under the grill until lightly toasted.

SINGING HINNY

Makes 12

Ingredients

- 225g/8oz plain flour
- 110g/4oz butter, diced
- 30g/1oz currants
- 120ml/4fl oz milk
- 60ml/2fl oz soured cream
- ½ tsp salt
- 1 tsp baking powder

Preparation method

Preheat a griddle or bakestone.

In a large bowl, sift the flour and add the butter, rubbing together with your fingertips until it resembles breadcrumbs. Add the currants, milk, cream, salt and baking powder, and stir well to form a dough. Add a splash of milk if necessary.

On a lightly-floured work surface, roll out the dough to a 2cm/1in thickness, and cut into 8cm/3in rounds.

Cook the cakes for 2–3 mins on each side, or until golden brown.

SOMERSET CIDER CAKE

Serves 6–8

Ingredients

- 350ml/12fl oz cider
- 150g/5oz dark brown sugar
- 150g/5oz butter, melted
- 4 cooking apples, peeled and grated
- 2 eggs, beaten
- 300g/11oz plain flour
- 2 tsp baking soda
- 1 tsp mixed spice
- 1 tsp ground cinnamon
- pinch of freshly grated nutmeg
- 200g/7oz golden sultanas
- 110g/4oz chopped pecans

Preparation method

Preheat the oven to 180C/350F/Gas 4. Grease a 20cm/8in easy-release or springform cake tin.

Boil the cider in a small pan over a medium heat until reduced by two-thirds.

In a large bowl, beat together the sugar and butter until light and fluffy. Add the grated apple, eggs and cider, and stir well.

In a separate bowl, sift the flour and add the baking soda, mixed spice, cinnamon and nutmeg. Stir well, then pour in the cider and apple mixture. Fold in the sultanas and pecans, and stir.

Transfer to the cake tin and bake for 50–60 mins.

SPOTTED DICK

Serves 6–8

Ingredients

- 300g/11oz plain flour
- 2 tsp baking powder
- 150g/5oz shredded suet
- 75g/3oz caster sugar
- 110g/4oz currants
- zest of 1 lemon
- 200ml/7fl oz milk

Preparation method

In a large bowl, sift the flour and add baking powder, suet, sugar, currants and lemon zest, and mix well. Gradually add the milk, stirring well to form a dough. Grease a pudding basin. Transfer the dough into the basin, and cover with baking paper. Tie a piece of string around the edge to hold the paper in place, then place a damp tea towel on top and tie again to secure it in place.

Place the pudding basin in a large saucepan, filling two-thirds with cold water. Cover, bring to the boil, and simmer for 1 hr.

STICKY TOFFEE PUDDING

Serves 4

Ingredients

For the sponge
- 300ml/10fl oz tea
- 225g/8oz dates, chopped
- 110g/4oz butter
- 175g/6oz demerara sugar
- 3 eggs, beaten
- 225g/8oz self-raising flour
- 1 tsp bicarbonate of soda
- 1 tsp vanilla extract

For the sauce
- 110g/4oz butter
- 175g/6oz demerara sugar

- 110g/4oz caster sugar
- 275g/10oz golden syrup
- 225ml/8fl oz double cream
- 1 tsp vanilla essence

Preparation method

Preheat the oven to 180C/350F/Gas 4. Grease an ovenproof dish.

Pour the tea into a large bowl, then add the dates, and allow to cool for 15 mins.

Beat the butter and sugar in a separate bowl, then gradually add the eggs. Sift in the flour, bicarbonate of soda, vanilla extract, and stir until combined and smooth. Pour in the date and tea mixture and combine. Transfer the mixture to the dish, and bake for 60–90 mins.

Meanwhile, heat the butter, demerara and caster sugar and syrup in a small pan over a low heat, whisking continuously. Remove from the heat and stir in the cream and vanilla essence. Return to the heat for a further 2–3 mins until smooth.

Pour the sauce over the sponge and serve warm.

Blessed be he that invented
the pudding – to come in
pudding time is to come to
the most lucky moment in
the world.

Francis Maximilian Misson

… and what is literature compared with cooking? One is shadow and the other is substance.

E. V. Lucas, *Rose and Rose*

SUSSEX POND PUDDING

Serves 6

Ingredients

For the pastry
- 225g/8oz self-raising flour
- 110g/4oz shredded suet
- 90ml/3fl oz milk
- 60ml/2fl oz water

For the filling
- 200g/7oz light brown sugar
- 200g/7oz butter, diced
- 2 large lemons

Preparation method

Grease a 1½ litre/53fl oz pudding basin.

In a large bowl, sift the flour and mix in the suet. Gradually pour in the milk and water together, stirring continuously to form a dough.

Leave aside a quarter of the dough to be used later. On a lightly-floured work surface, roll out the dough to form a large round. Use this to line the pudding basin:

Pour half of the sugar and half of the diced butter into the bottom of the pudding basin. Use a skewer to make several holes through the lemons. Place them in the pudding basin, then top up with the remaining butter and sugar.

Use the remaining pastry to form a round lid, pressing the edges together to seal. Place baking paper over the top of the basin, and then cover with aluminium foil. Use string to secure.

Boil the basin in a large, covered pan for 3–4 hrs, topping up the water to come half way up the basin throughout the cooking.

TEA LOAF

Serves 6–8

Ingredients

- 75g/3oz raisins
- 75g/3oz sultanas
- 75g/3oz currants
- 300ml/10fl oz tepid tea
- 250g/9oz self-raising flour
- 200g/7oz light brown sugar
- 1 egg, beaten
- 1 tsp ground cinnamon
- 1 tsp freshly grated nutmeg

Preparation method

Soak the raisins, sultanas and currants in the tea overnight in a covered bowl.

The next day, preheat the oven to 170C/330F/Gas 3. Grease a 23cm x 10cm/9in x 4in loaf tin.

Stir the fruit mix, then sift in the flour and add the sugar, egg, cinnamon and nutmeg to the bowl. Stir well, then transfer to the loaf tin.

Bake for 75 mins.

TREACLE TART

Serves 6–8

Ingredients

For the pastry

- 225g/8oz plain flour
- 110g/4oz butter, diced
- 1 egg, beaten
- 1 tbsp cold water

For the filling

- 450g/1lb golden syrup
- 75g/3oz fresh breadcrumbs
- pinch of ground ginger (optional)
- zest of 1 lemon, grated
- juice of ½ lemon

Preparation method

In a large bowl, sift the flour and add the butter, rubbing together using your fingertips. Fold in the egg to form a dough, adding water if necessary.

On a lightly-floured work surface, knead the dough until smooth.

Line a 23cm/9in tart tin with the dough, prick the base with a fork, and chill in the fridge for 30 mins.

Preheat the oven to 190C/375F/Gas 5.

Line the pastry with baking paper, fill with baking beans, and bake for 15 mins. Remove the baking paper and beans and return to the oven for a further 5 mins, or until golden brown.

In a large bowl, combine the syrup, breadcrumbs, ginger, lemon zest and juice, then pour into the pastry case. Bake for 30 mins.

VANILLA AND BLACKBERRY CHEESECAKE

Serves 6–8

Ingredients

For the cheesecake base

- 200g/7oz digestive biscuits
- 50g/2oz butter

For the cheesecake filling

- seeds of 1 vanilla pod
- 500g/1lb 2oz full-fat cream cheese
- 3 eggs, beaten
- juice of ½ lemon
- 90ml/3fl oz double cream

- 50g/2oz plain flour
- 200g/7oz caster sugar

For the blackberry purée
- 110g/4oz blackberries
- 2 tsp caster sugar

Preparation method

Preheat the oven to 130C/250F/Gas ½. Grease a 20cm/8in easy-release or springform cake tin and line with baking paper.

Grind the digestive biscuits until they resemble breadcrumbs. Gently heat the butter until melted, then mix in with the biscuits. Transfer the mixture into the cake tin, and press down with the bottom of a glass to compact and even it out. Chill in the fridge for 30 mins.

To make the cheesecake filling, beat the vanilla seeds and cream cheese in a large bowl until combined, then add the eggs, lemon juice and cream. Stir well. Add the flour and sugar, and continue to stir until smooth. Transfer to the cake tin.

To make the purée, gently heat the blackberries and sugar until the sugar is melted and the berries soften.

Use a blender to form a smooth purée, straining if necessary, then pour this on top of the cheesecake.
Bake for 40 mins, then allow to cool completely before removing from the tin.

… she knew, and we knew, and she knew that we knew, and we knew that she knew that we knew, she had been busy all the morning making tea-bread and sponge-cakes.

Elizabeth Gaskell, *Cranford*

VICTORIA SPONGE

Serves 10–12

Ingredients

For the cake
- 225g/8oz butter
- 225g/8oz caster sugar
- 4 eggs
- 2 tsp vanilla extract
- 225g/8oz self-raising flour
- 1 tbsp milk

For the filling
- jam and/or whipped cream

To serve
- caster sugar

Preparation method

Preheat the oven to 180C/350F/Gas 4. Grease two 18cm/7in cake tins and line with baking paper.

Beat the butter and the sugar in a bowl until they are light and fluffy. Beat in the eggs and vanilla extract.

Fold in the flour, adding milk if needed, to make the batter.

Divide the mixture between the cake tins and use a spatula to create a smooth surface.

Bake for 20–25 mins, or until golden-brown.

Remove from the oven and leave to stand for 5 mins.

Remove from the tin and peel off the paper, placing on a wire rack to cool completely.

Spread jam or whipped cream (or both!) onto the top of one of the cakes, and then place the second on top to form a sandwich. Dust with caster sugar.

WELSH CAKES

Makes 6

Ingredients

- 225g/8oz self-raising flour
- 110g/4oz butter, diced
- 75g/3oz caster sugar
- 25g/1oz sultanas
- 1 egg, beaten
- 1 tbsp milk

Preparation method

Preheat a griddle or bakestone.

In a large bowl, sift the flour and add the butter, rubbing together with your fingertips until it resembles breadcrumbs. Add the sugar, sultanas and egg and stir well to form a dough. Add a splash of milk if necessary. On a lightly-floured work surface, roll out the dough to a 5mm/½in thickness, and cut into 10cm/4in rounds. Cook the cakes for 2–3 mins on each side, or until golden brown, then dust with caster sugar.

WELSH HARVEST CAKE

Serves 10–12

Ingredients

- 175g/6oz butter
- 175g/6oz brown sugar
- 2 eggs, beaten
- 225g/8oz self-raising flour
- ½ tsp mixed spice
- ½ tsp ground cinnamon
- 450g/1lb cooking apples, peeled, cored and diced
- 50g/2oz sultanas
- 50g/2oz currants
- 50g/2oz flaked almonds

Preparation method

Preheat the oven to 180C/350F/Gas 4. Grease an 18cm/7in cake tin and line with baking paper.

In a small pan, gently melt the butter and sugar, then remove from the heat. Add the eggs and beat to combine.

In a large bowl, sift the flour, mixed spice and cinnamon, then pour in the melted butter mix. Stir well.

In a separate bowl, mix the apples, sultanas, currants and almonds together.

Transfer half the mixture into the cake tin. Pour the fruit mix on top, and then top with the remaining cake mixture.

Bake for 55–60 mins. Place on a wire rack and allow to cool completely.

www.summersdale.com